KEEP YOUR
DREAMS
Alive
dream catcher
coloring books
for adults

COLORING BOOKS FOR ADULTS

This Book
belongs to

COLOR
TEST PAGE

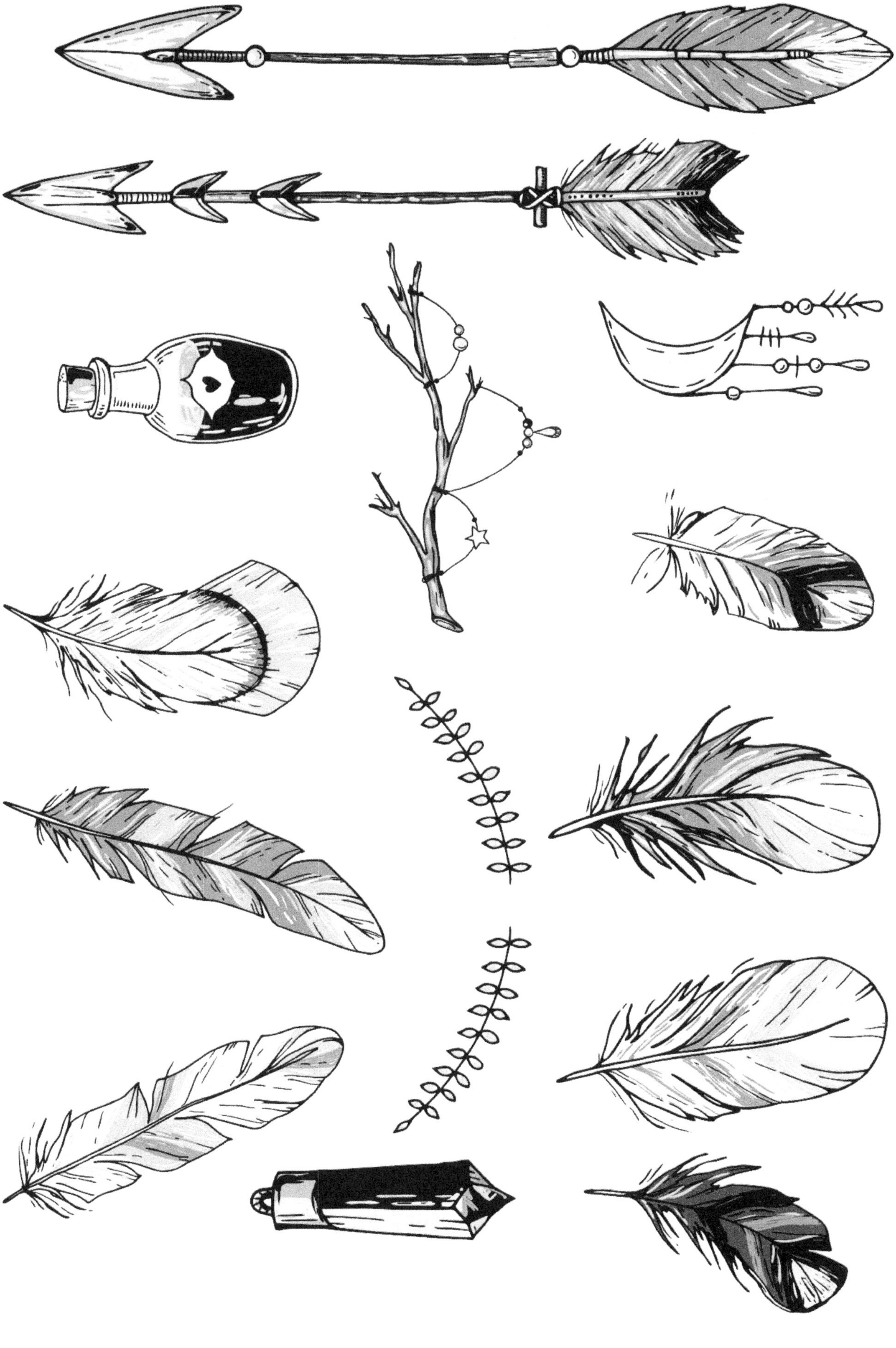

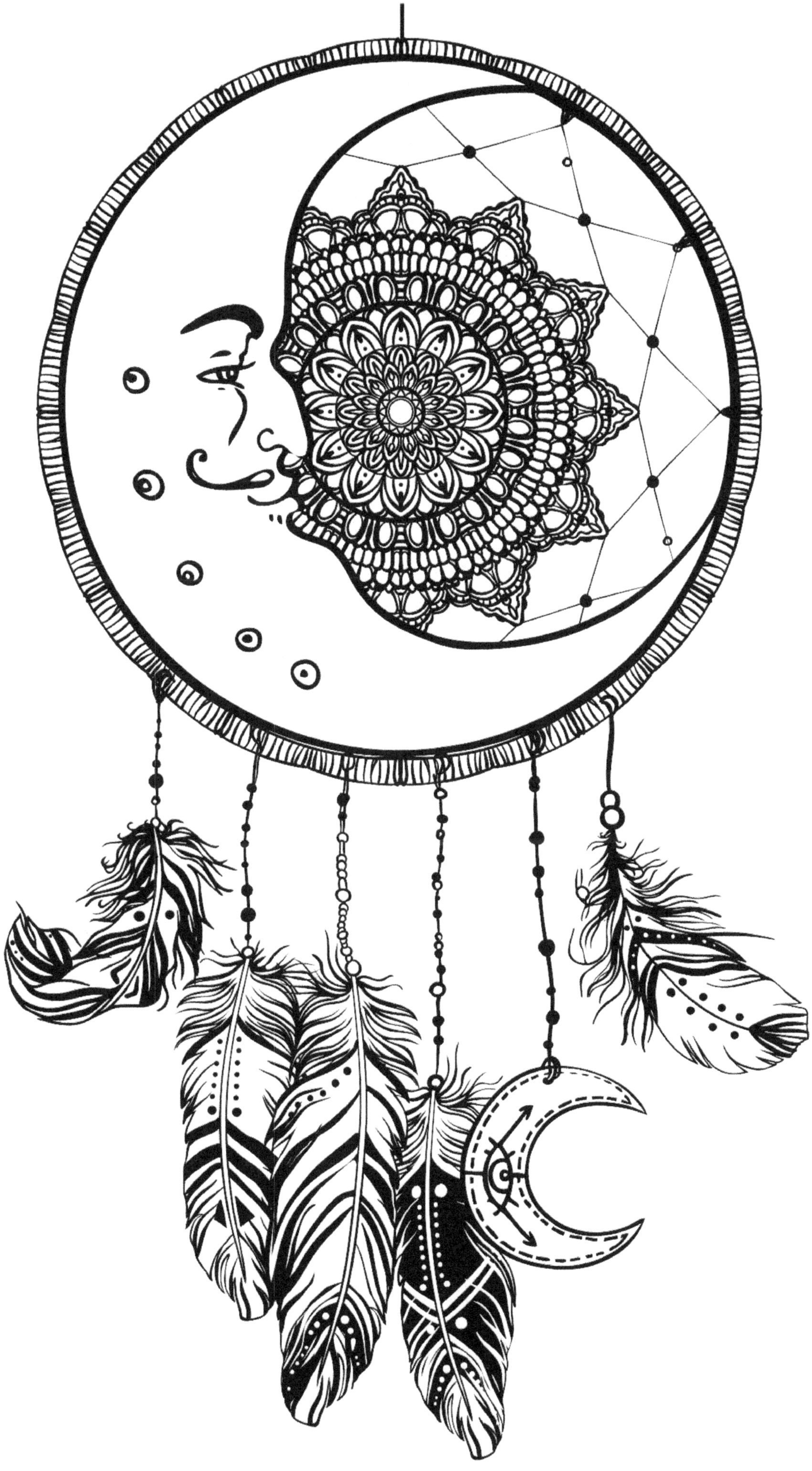

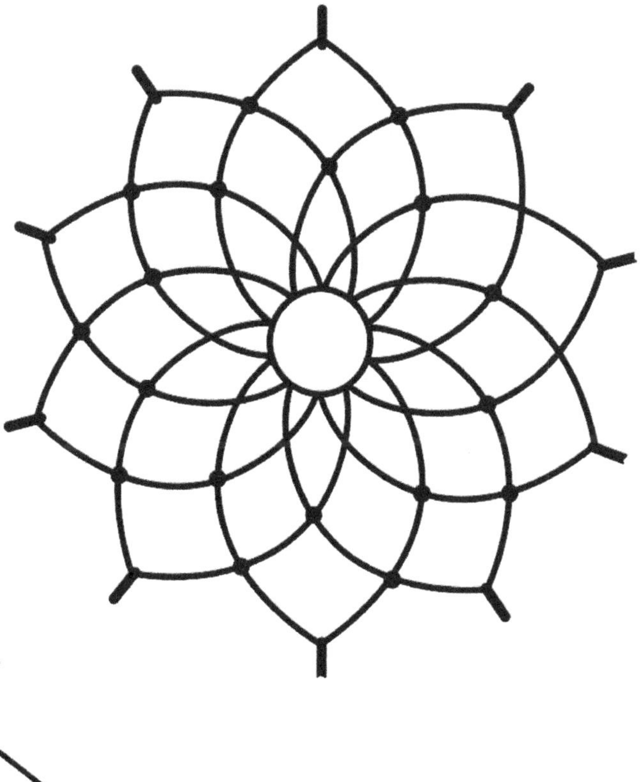

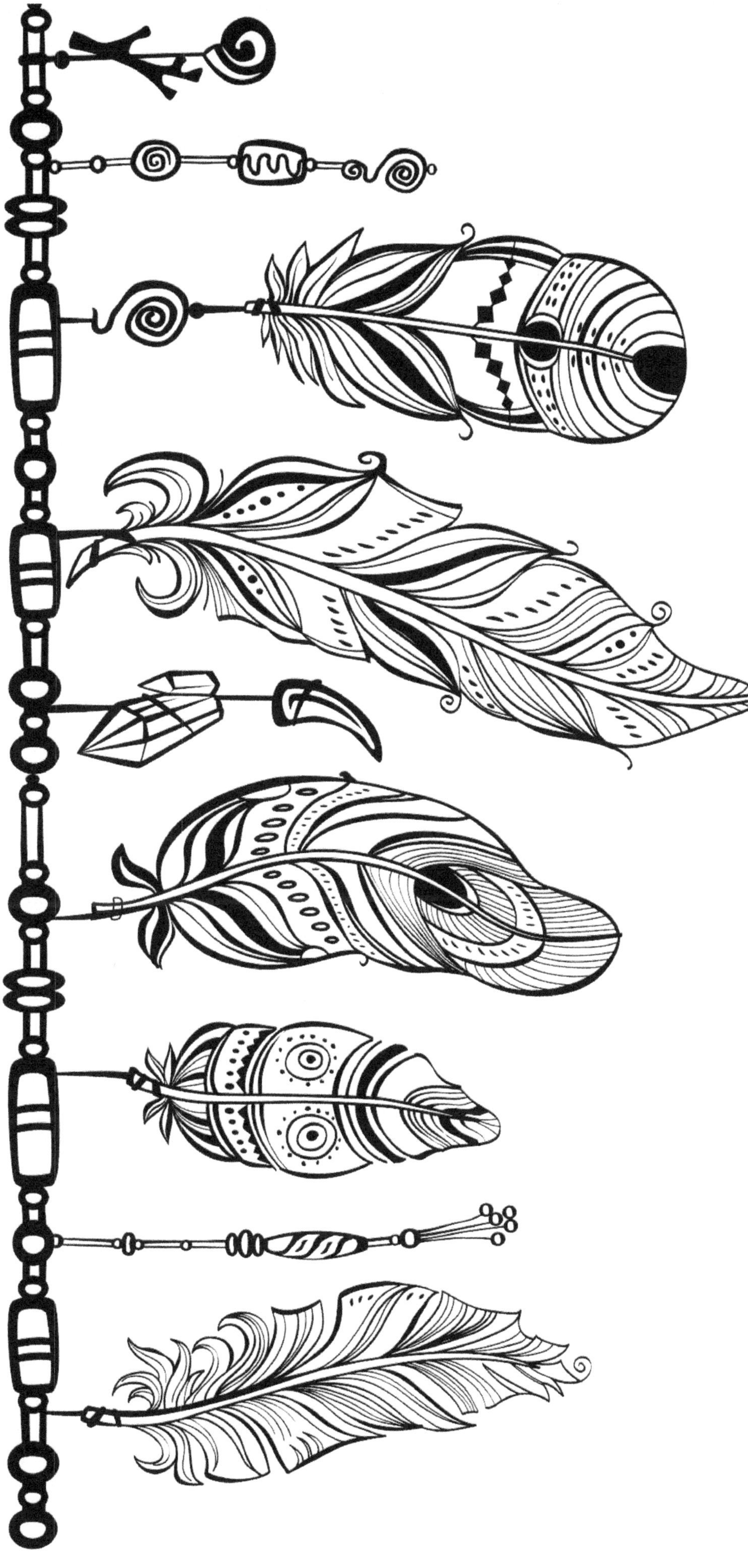

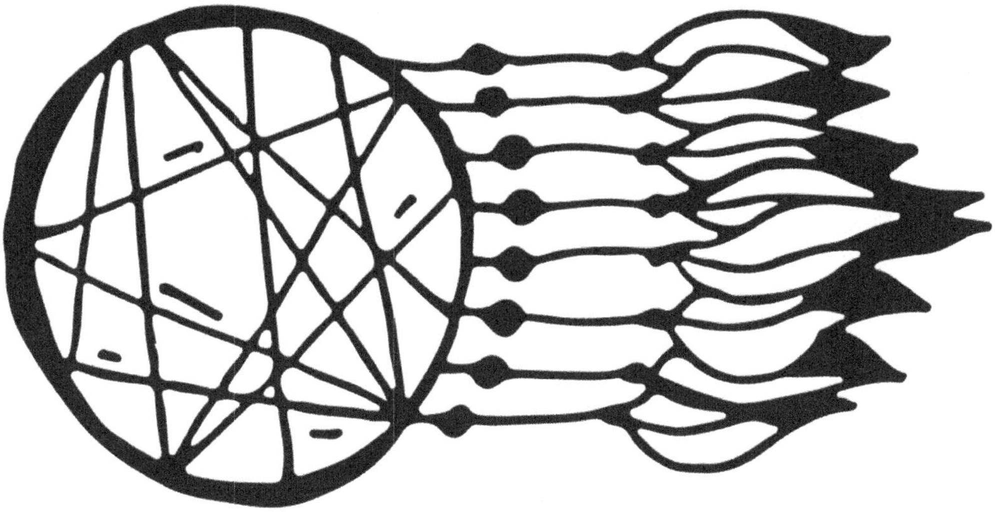

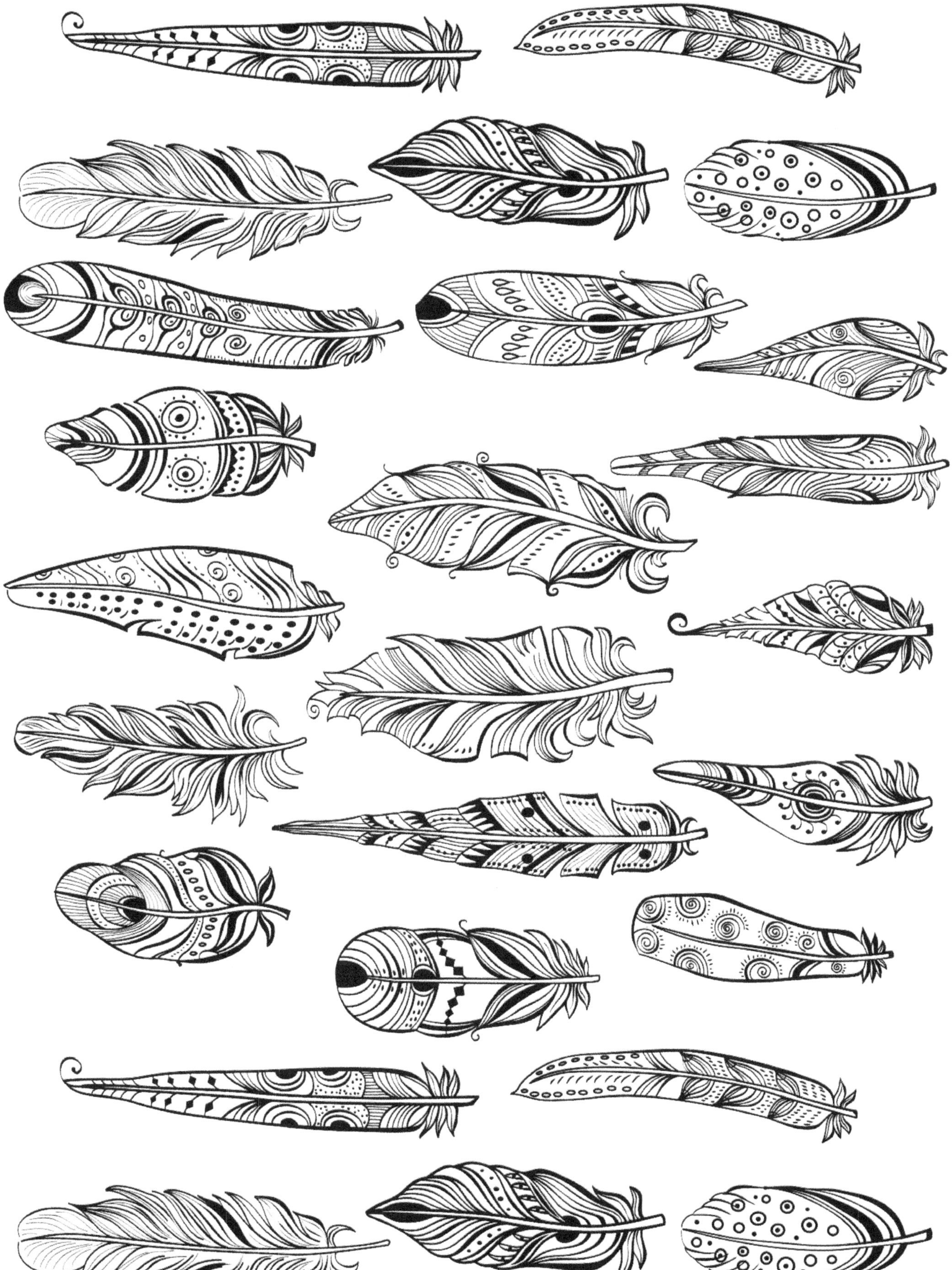

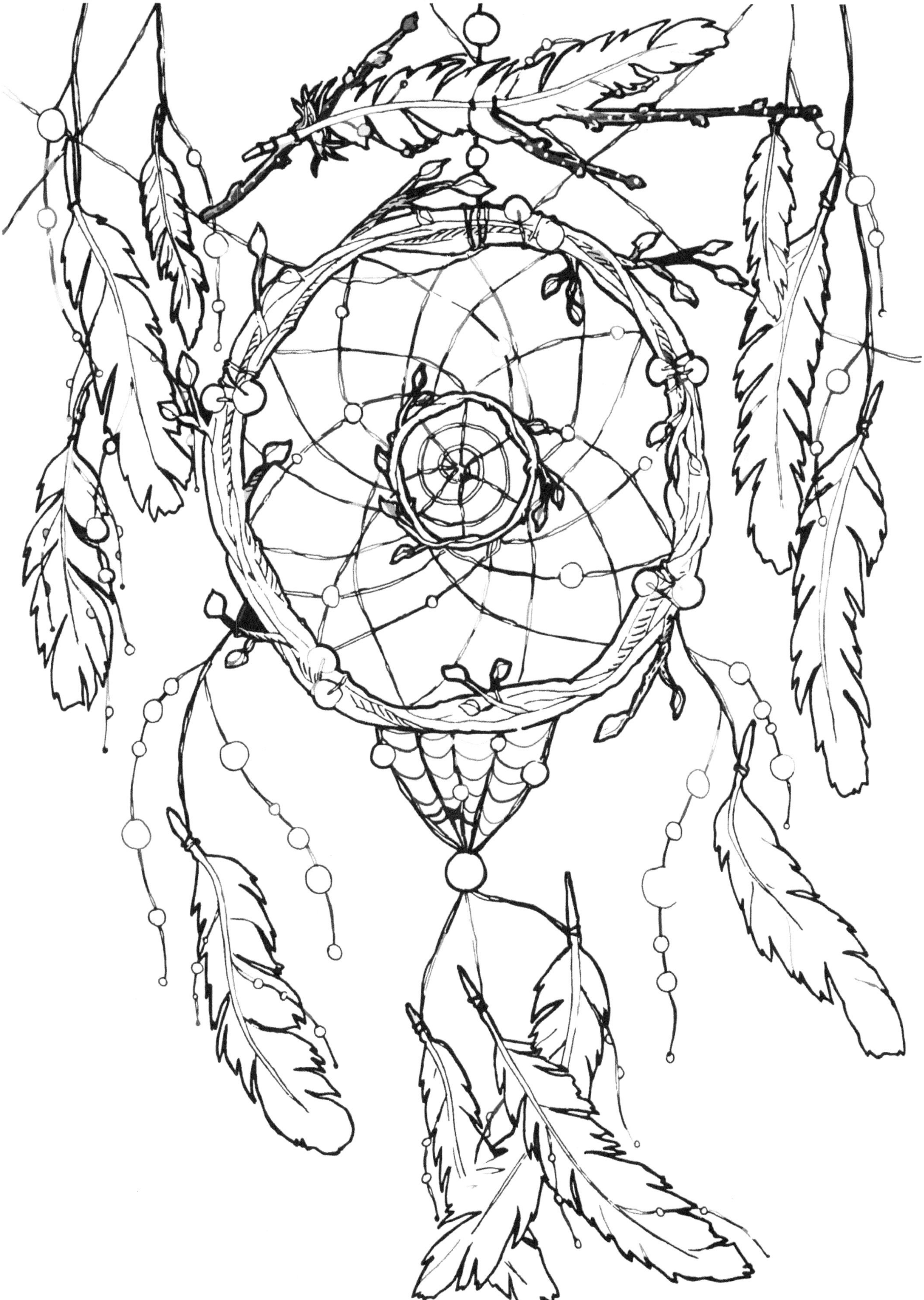

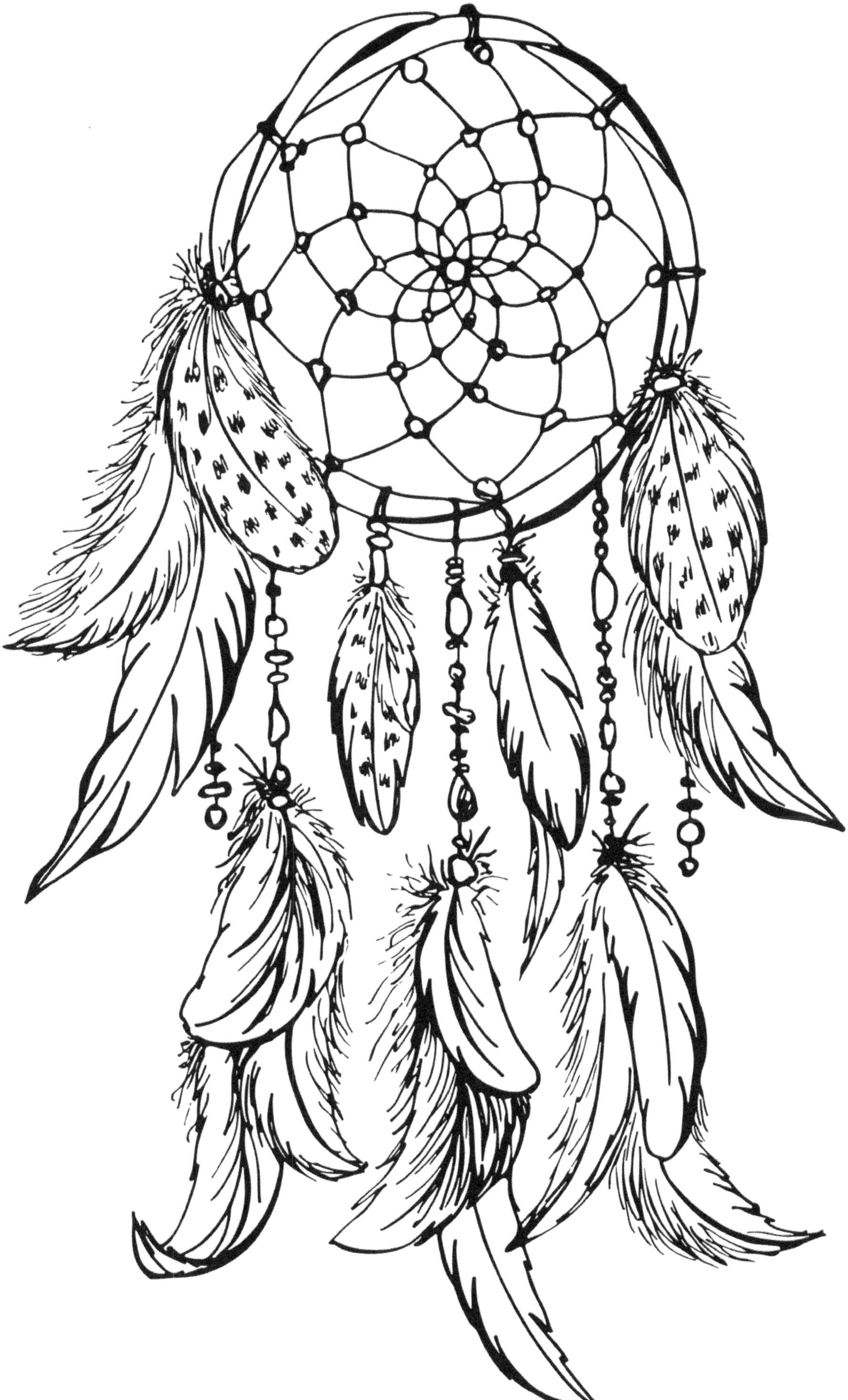

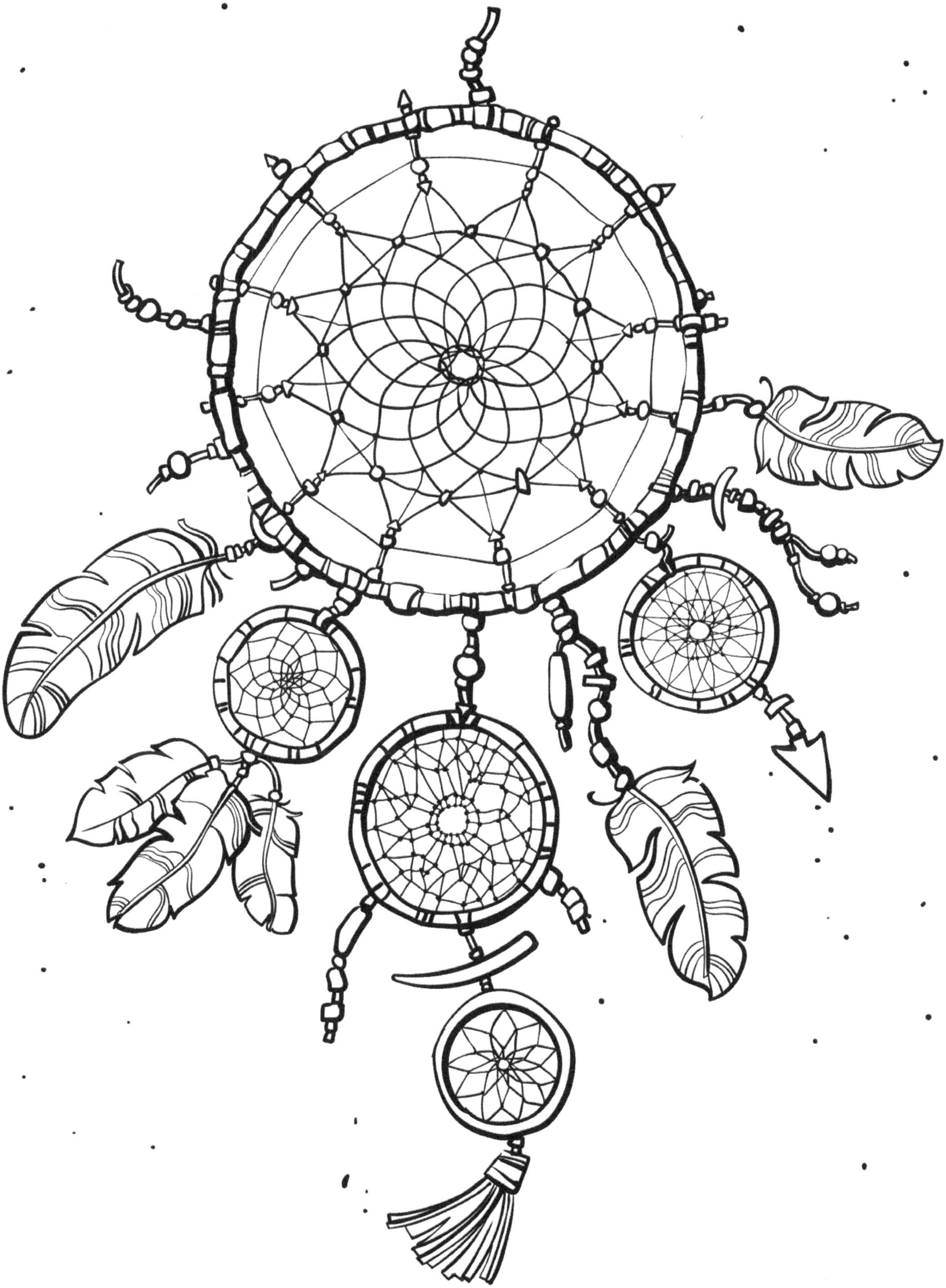

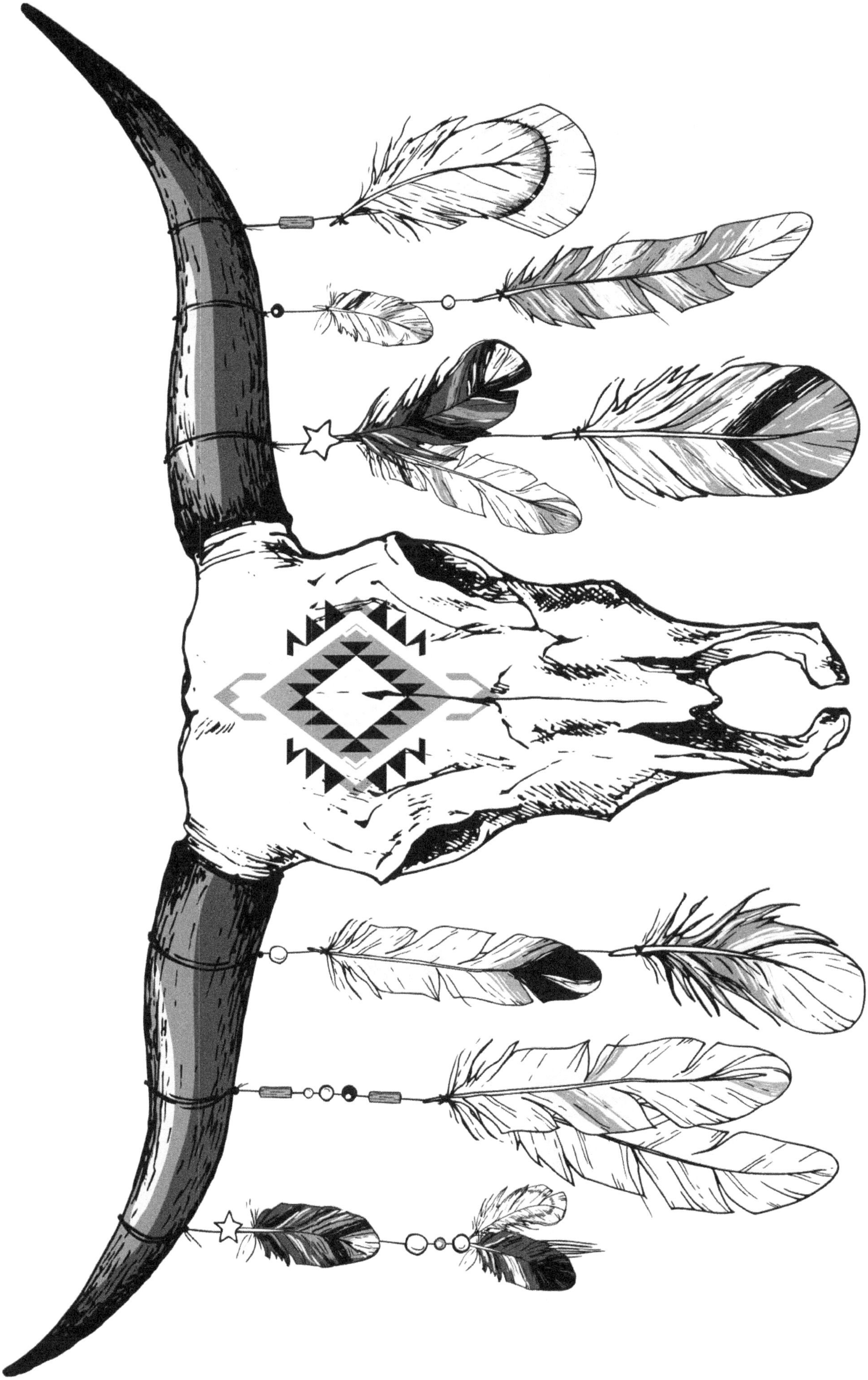

Made in the USA
Las Vegas, NV
17 September 2021

30480747R00044